"F … g direction…
a … remarkable
ab … et entirely in
S … yes, but we
… rly."

"A … ng art form.
…F … rformances of
un … s not only to
the … n one as well."

… project,

… dness
… s…"

Nominated for Five Dora Mavor Moore Awards, including:
Outstanding Production
Outstanding New Play
Outstanding Direction (Daryl Cloran)
Outstanding Performance (Holly Lewis)
Outstanding Set Design (Lorenzo Savoini)

RETURN

THE SARAJEVO PROJECT

PRODUCED BY THEATREFRONT

RETURN

(The Sarajevo Project)

PRODUCED BY THEATREFRONT

created by Sue Balint, Daryl Cloran,
Alena Džebo, Holly Lewis, Christopher Morris,
Tanja Smoje and Dylan Trowbridge

Playwrights Canada Press
Toronto • Canada

Playwrights Canada Press
The Canadian Drama Publisher
215 Spadina Avenue, Suite 230, Toronto, Ontario CANADA M5T 2C7
416-703-0013 fax 416-408-3402
orders@playwrightscanada.com • www.playwrightscanada.com

Financial support provided by the taxpayers of Canada and Ontario through the Canada Council for the Arts and the Department of Canadian Heritage through the Book Publishing Industry Development Programme, and the Ontario Arts Council.

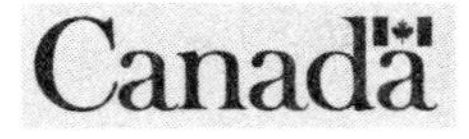

Front cover image and design by Elliott Smith.
Production Editor: JLArt

Library and Archives Canada Cataloguing in Publication

Return : (the Sarajevo project) / produced by Theatrefront.

ISBN 978-0-88754-725-6

1. Yugoslav War, 1991-1995--Refugees--Drama. 2. Yugoslav War, 1991-1995--Drama. 3. Sarajevo (Bosnia and Hercegovina)--Drama. I. Theatrefront (Theater group) II. Title: Sarajevo project.

PS8600.R48 2007 C812'.6 C2007-900672-8

First edition: April 2007.
Printed and bound by AGMV Marquis at Quebec, Canada.

Contents

Acknowledgements

Special thanks to all of the theatre artists (both Bosnian and Canadian) who participated in the numerous phases of development for this project, your contributions have been invaluable.

Thank you to Faruk Lončarević, without whom our development workshop in Sarajevo could never have happened.

Thank you to the Tarragon Theatre for its support of this project through the Workspace Program. And special thanks to both Andy McKim and Richard Rose for their advice and dramaturgy.

Thank you to Ms. Gordana Bosanac at the Canadian Embassy in Sarajevo who provided us with support and assistance throughout the creation process.

Thanks also to Mladen Ovadija, Biljana Ovadija, Jelena Ovadija, Perla Ovadija-Mosca, Antonio Mosca, Minka, Barbara Andrade, Sabrina Fursman, Mima Bulodic, Sasha Lukac, Bruce Beaton and Gillian Gallow.

And of course, thank you to the Canada Council for the Arts, the Ontario Arts Council, the Toronto Arts Council and the Laidlaw Foundation for their support of the various stages of development.

Introduction

March 7, 2003

Sitting on the floor in my Sarajevo flat. I have about half an hour to write before I have to leave for rehearsal. Part of me wants to sob and spend this half hour complaining and struggling with the meaning of my life. Part of me wants to flick through my memories of Dubrovnik; white marble, orange trees, the blue-green of the Adriatic. And another part of me wants to blast through the Sarajevo project, trying to piece together what we are trying to do here. What have we accomplished? Where do we go from here?

We came to Sarajevo to learn and to be inspired by theatre artists from a different culture. We wanted to make a story, with people, to discover what we had in common and we hoped that very act of storytelling would begin to build a bridge. "[We] launch'd forth filament, filament, filament, out of [ourselves] … Till the bridge [we] will need be form'd…" *

What is our need to connect? Why are we here?

Today, in rehearsal, we are having a vote. We have to make a choice between two directions to go with the project. After today, we will either continue forward with seven separate stories connected together by the idea of slaughtered innocence (based on the legend of the seven brothers) or with a story about a brother returning home after 10 years. If the vote fails to produce one united group how will we continue?

Well. That's half an hour. I have to head off to the Bosnian National Theatre. Not a bad way to live my life, really.

• • •

I wrote the preceding passage in my journal one week before the first public presentation of *The Sarajevo Project*. The vote succeeded in uniting the group to create a story of a brother returning home, which has culminated in the play that appears in printed form in this book.

* Walt Whitman, "A Noiseless Patient Spider"

RETURN (The Sarajevo Project) is the product of a three-year creation process between 21 artists in two countries. The idea for the project began as a change of direction for Theatrefront in 2002. Daryl Cloran called a meeting. It was a kind of State of the Union. Theatrefront had been created as an ensemble of theatre artists with a mandate to provide an environment for theatre professionals to take dramatic risks, to push themselves to new emotional and physical limits. This objective had resulted in productions of challenging contemporary works and sold-out performances. But to risk, to innovate, we needed a change of direction. This is the reason Daryl had gathered us all together that night.

We sat in a circle in the living room of an apartment just off College Street in Toronto's Little Italy. Folded in an overstuffed couch, perched on stools and even lining the floor, we drank wine and talked about how we would begin. The company agreed that Daryl's challenge would be best met by working internationally.

This is where we began. Ensemble member Christopher Morris was out of the blocks first. Interested in creating a production with actors from Sarajevo, he put on his backpack, and with the name of one contact in his pocket, he jumped on a plane to Bosnia. After 3 weeks, he met a young director in a bar in the basement of the Acting Academy in Sarajevo. This young director was Faruk Lončarević, who became the first member of our Sarajevo team.

Faruk assembled three Bosnian actors and Theatrefront flew three Canadian actors, a writer and a director to Sarajevo to work together for five weeks. We started with nothing but ourselves (our histories, our belief in theatre, and our imagined futures), and together we began to build a play. It was a huge undertaking for a small independent company. I remember our producer, Claire Sakaki, handing Daryl the cheque for five flights to Sarajevo saying, "Please bring home a play."

The process led to a bi-national play that was the product of three phases of international collaboration. The first phase took place in Bosnia and involved direct intercultural exchange (sharing stories, language, dance and songs). It culminated in a public presentation of the material we had developed, a loose collection of scenes, which served as the backbone for the full-length play we eventually created. The second phase took place in Toronto and was co-produced by the Tarragon Theatre as part of its Workspace Play Development Program. The artists from both countries continued to develop the play towards a full production through improvisation and scene writing. The third phase was an extended development/rehearsal period in Toronto at the end of which we presented the world premiere of the production.

RETURN (The Sarajevo Project) is the product of an experiment in building cultural bridges. It is the culmination of trust, risk and a great deal of effort. However, in the end it is the connection with the audience that is the true test of a piece of theatre, and sharing our collaboration with the audience was the greatest risk. On the opening night of the premiere of the play, waiting backstage as the lights dimmed and the call to prayer played (a sound we had heard for the first time together, floating over the old Turkish Quarter in Sarajevo), we held our breaths and together we began the play.

Holly Lewis
Theatrefront Ensemble Member

The initial workshop of *The Sarajevo Project* took place in Sarajevo between February 17 and March 12, 2003. Its first public performance was on March 12, 2003 at the CDA Theatre as part of the Sarajevo Winter Festival, with the following company:

Elma Ahmetović	Lejla
Alena Džebo	Jasna
Patricia Fagan	Sarah
Holly Lewis	Gypsy Child
Sanin Milavić	Emir / Zlatan
Christopher Morris	Tarik / Meša

Directors: Daryl Cloran and Faruk Lončarević
Dramaturge: Sue Balint

• • •

Theatrefront held a second workshop of the material in Toronto in May 2003, concluding with a public presentation of two scenes at the Tarragon Theatre's Spring Arts Fair on June 1, with the following company:

Damien Atkins	Noah / Woman on tram
Holly Lewis	Lejla / Woman on tram
Matthew MacFadzean	Emir / Zlatan
Christopher Morris	Tarik / Meša
Michelle Polak	Jasna / Sarah

Director: Daryl Cloran
Dramaturge: Sue Balint

• • •

In January 2004 a third workshop was co-produced by Theatrefront and the Tarragon Theatre with the following company:

Sanela Babić	Lejla
Alena Džebo	Jasna / Elma's Mother
Holly Lewis	Sarah / Elma
Christopher Morris	Tarik / Meša
Emir Zec	Emir / Zlatan / UN Soldier

Director: Daryl Cloran
Dramaturge: Sue Balint
Stage Manager: Thom Payne
Assistant Director: Brendon Allen

The premiere of *RETURN (The Sarajevo Project)* was produced at the Tarragon Theatre Extra Space from January 10–29, 2006 with the following company:

Alena Džebo	Jasna / Old Woman
Holly Lewis	Sarah / Elma
Christopher Morris	Tarik
Tanja Smoje	Lejla
Dylan Trowbridge	Emir / UN Soldier

Director: Daryl Cloran
Producer: Claire Sakaki
Associate Producer: Kaija Robinson
Dramaturge: Sue Balint
Costume Designer: Dana Osborne
Set and Lighting Designer: Lorenzo Savoini
Music and Sound Designer: Lyon Smith
Stage Manager: Trina Sookhai
Production Manager: Ryan McDougall
Apprentice Stage Manager: Liz Shefield
Assistant Director: Alison Williams

Characters

Tarik Nakaš
Sarah Nakaš
Emir Nakaš
Lejla Nakaš
Jasna
Elma
*The cast doubles as secondary characters where necessary.

Setting

TARIK and SARAH visit Sarajevo in the autumn of 1998.
TARIK's wartime memories flash back to 1993.

The Nakaš flat serves as the hub of activity and will require a table and three chairs. Stage directions suggest the flat has 3 bedrooms, a kitchen and bathroom. The characters also spend time on a balcony off the main room, presumably with a view of the city.

Notes

Officially, the siege of Sarajevo lasted from April 1992 until December 14, 1995. However, in the spring of 1998, approximately 30,000 SFOR (Stabilisation Force) troops were still active in the city.

[Translations appear throughout the script in square brackets.]

RETURN
(The Sarajevo Project)

Prologue: Sniper's Alley, Spring 1993

Lights up on the alley.

Sporadic gunfire continues throughout the scene.

TARIK stands at the edge of the alley. A man appears beside him. Both of them carry water canisters. The man sprints through the alley avoiding gunfire, then exits.

ELMA enters without a canister.

ELMA Tarik!

TARIK *Elma. Lejla te čeka.* [Elma. Lejla's waiting for you.]

ELMA *Lejla.*

TARIK *Kod nas. Trebaš vodu? Gdje ti je kanister. Ja ću—* [Back at our place. You need water? Where is your canister? I'll—]

ELMA *Ne Tarik... (showing him an envelope) Vidi ovo? Starci su mi nabavili lovu... deset hiljada.* [No Tarik.... See this? My parents got the money... ten thousand.]

TARIK *Šta?* [What?]

Two women enter with their canisters and begin crossing. Another round of gunfire. One woman freezes with fear. Everyone yells at her to keep going. The first woman doubles back, grabs the frozen woman, they complete their crossing and exit.

ELMA *Idem do cisterne, i oni će me izvući van.* [I'm getting on the water truck over there and they're taking me out.]

TARIK *Gdje ideš?* [Where?]

ELMA *Ne znam. Pozdravi mi Lejlu. Reci joj da sam u redu.* [I don't know. Tell Lejla goodbye. Tell her I'm safe.]

TARIK *Hoću, naravno. Elma, čuvaj se.* [I will, of course. Elma, be careful.]

ELMA *Poželi mi sreću.* [Wish me luck.]

TARIK *Sretno.* [Good luck.]

ELMA runs out into the alley. Another round of shots are fired. ELMA falls, dropping the envelope beside her.

Elma!

Blackout. The sound of coins falling.

Scene One

Lights up on the Grave of the Seven Brothers.

1998. TARIK and SARAH have just arrived in Sarajevo and still have their luggage with them.

SARAH Tarik?

TARIK Look at this place. Nothing is like I remember it.

SARAH Your family will be. Five years is nothing for brothers and sisters.

TARIK Sarah, will you marry me?

SARAH I already did. Yes! And again *(kiss)* and again *(kiss)* and again. *(kiss)*

TARIK And again.

SARAH I should have learned more Bosnian. All I'm going to be able to say all week is "*Zdravo, Ja sam Sarah Nakaš.*" [Hello, I am Sarah Nakaš.]

TARIK It'll be fine. Emir speaks English. This park used to be full of trees. In the winter, before the war I used to walk around making paths for Lejla to follow home in the snow. I used to try and trick her, leave footprints on either side of the trunk so it looked like I'd walked right through the tree. There were so many trees.

SARAH What happened to them?

TARIK We started cutting them for firewood. The first winter was very cold. Emir and I came out together once in the night to find branches to burn. There was a little white dog. Emir wanted to take him home. A ratty little dog. I've got to get them out of here.

SARAH Your family is going to be so surprised!

TARIK *(kneels and speaks to her tummy)* They're going to be surprised about you too, my *majmunčiću*. [little monkey.]

SARAH starts to walk.

Wait, wait. Do you feel it?

SARAH What?

TARIK This is a sacred space. Do you feel it?

SARAH A little. I think. I've got the chills.

TARIK This is the grave I told you about. The Grave of the Seven Brothers.

SARAH Oh my God.

TARIK Do you want to?

SARAH Can we?

TARIK I think we have to.

SARAH Are there really dead people in there?

TARIK Take these coins. Ask your question, say your prayer at each door, put a coin in each slot—

SARAH And the first words I hear are the answer to my question.

TARIK I'll go first.

TARIK goes first, SARAH follows behind. They go past the graves, dropping a coin and praying at each one. TARIK finishes his prayers and listens as pedestrians cross past him silently.

At the last grave, SARAH realizes she's out of coins. She double-checks her pockets, prays extra hard and walks to TARIK.

SARAH You made a mistake.

TARIK registers his "first words."

Oh no, you haven't heard anything yet! So what I just said was your first—

TARIK What happened?

SARAH I didn't have enough money, you said seven brothers but there's eight doors.

TARIK There's seven brothers and the eighth door is the entrance.

SARAH But you only gave me seven coins.

TARIK Look *(digging in his pockets)* just go back and put this in the last one.

SARAH That's all right?

TARIK It's fine, it's fine, just circle back around.

SARAH circles back to the last grave, makes her wish again and drops the last coin. The pedestrians cross, speaking in Bosnian, and exit.

SARAH What did they say? What did I hear?

TARIK Well, that guy was supposed to meet her at six...

SARAH ...six...

TARIK ...and she said something about her car.

SARAH Okay... a car... meeting someone at six, okay. What's that mean? That doesn't mean anything. What a rip-off. Oh, and I ruined yours. Pretend you didn't hear anything.

TARIK Okay.

SARAH I can fix it. *(whispers in his ear from behind)* Sarah loves you. That's it! That's all that matters. Right?

TARIK Right. Come on, Sarah, let's go. *(They start to walk.)* I can't wait to eat. Burek... pita... baklava... ćevapi!

SARAH I hope ćevapi is a big salad.

TARIK This way.

TARIK turns around the corner. Lights snap to Sniper's Alley flashback. The man sprints across as before.

SARAH Tarik?

Lights snap back to normal.

TARIK Not that way.

SARAH Should we call? Can you find your way home?

TARIK In the dark, the river is still here and the mountains.

SARAH Don't worry. C'mere. Your family is going to love Canada. I can't wait to show them our home.

TARIK *Kuća.* [Home.]

SARAH *Kuća.* I love it when you speak Bosnian… okay what's Bosnian for "I don't eat meat?"

TARIK I don't think that sentence has ever been spoken in the Balkans.

SARAH Oh come on.

TARIK *Ne jedem meso.*

SARAH *Ne jedem meso.* And… how do I say hero?

TARIK *Junak.*

SARAH Well you sir… are about to get a *junak*'s welcome.

TARIK We'll walk down my street and we'll see my house – it'll be just like I remembered it – you'll love it. And I'll push open the door and my sister…

SARAH Lejla!

LEJLA appears. She reacts as TARIK describes.

TARIK …will look at me and she won't be able to believe her eyes. Then she'll come to me, slowly and she'll reach out and touch my face, and give me a great big hug. And then she'll step back, look at me… and then she'll do it again. And then my little brother…

SARAH …Emir.

EMIR appears, reacts as TARIK describes.

TARIK He'll be so surprised. He won't know what to say – he'll slowly come to me – with his eyes so wide – like a kid who's never seen snow – I'll throw open my arms to him and he'll give me a great big…

EMIR punches him in the stomach.

LEJLA *Ne! Emire!*

Blackout.

Scene Two

Lights up on the main room of the Nakaš flat. SARAH stands by the door with the suitcases, still wearing her coat. TARIK sits at the table holding his stomach. LEJLA stares at him in disbelief.

LEJLA *Jesi li to ti?* [Is it really you?]

TARIK *Da, jesam.* [Yes, it's me.]

LEJLA *Šta… kako… tako si… ostario. Što nisi javio da dolaziš? Tvoj brat… u šoku je. Emire, dođi ovamo. Uvijek nešto izmišlja…* [What… how… you're so… you're an old man! You couldn't tell us you were coming? Your brother… your brother's in shock. Emir, come here. Always making things up…]

TARIK *Ovo je Sarah. Moja žena.* [This is Sarah. My wife.]

SARAH *Zdravo. Ja sam Sarah Nakaš.* [Hello. I am Sarah Nakaš.] It's so nice to finally meet you Lejla. *(to TARIK)* She doesn't speak English does she?

LEJLA *Zera… jesi Lijepa.* [Little… she's beautiful.]

SARAH Sarah—

LEJLA *Zera.* [Little.]

SARAH Sar-ah.

LEJLA *Zera.* [Little.]

SARAH Oh that's close…

TARIK Surprise! *Moj bože... ista si mama. (translating for SARAH)* She looks just like my mom.

LEJLA *Misliš?* [You think so?]

TARIK *Da.*

LEJLA *I Emir to kaže.* [Emir says so too.]

SARAH She looks like you too.

TARIK Don't tell her that.

SARAH Why? You're a very pretty man.

LEJLA *Šta?* [What?]

TARIK *Kaže da si sretna što ne ličiš na mene.* [She says you're lucky you don't look like me.]

She laughs dramatically for SARAH's benefit then begins to cry.

LEJLA *Gdje si bio?* [Where have you been?]

TARIK *U Kanadi.* [In Canada.]

LEJLA *Što se nisi javio? Gdje si bio?* [Why didn't you call? Where have you been?]

TARIK *Sjedi, sjedi, sjedi...* [Sit, sit, sit...] *(He takes immigration papers out to show her.) Lejla, da li bi željela doći u Kanadu?* [How would you like to come to Canada?] *Ovdje su svi papiri, za tebe i... Emira.* [Here are the papers for you and Emir.] We've arranged everything so you can both come back to Canada with us. *Vidi, tvoje ime, a ovo je za Emira.* [Look, your name and Emir's name.] We're sponsoring you. I've saved up the money. *Sve sam sredio, vi samo potpišite.* [Everything's ready, just sign.]

LEJLA *Za mene? I Emira?* [My name? And Emir's?]

TARIK *Da,* when you come, we have a room for both of you! *Imam kuću...* [I have a house...]

LEJLA reaches out and gently covers TARIK's mouth.

LEJLA Tarik, ssshhh...

TARIK *Imam pare.* [I have money.]

LEJLA Tarik…

TARIK *Potpiši.* [Sign.]

LEJLA Tarik Tarik Tarik…

LEJLA looks down at TARIK's feet and notices his shoes.

LEJLA *Tarik. Cipele.* [Shoes.]

TARIK Ah, our shoes. *Izvini, izvini…* sorry, sorry…

SARAH Oh sorry, sorry.

TARIK takes off his shoes and puts them over by the door. SARAH does the same.

(to TARIK) Are they still coming home with us?

TARIK Of course.

LEJLA *Vratio si se?* [Are you really back?]

TARIK *Da*, I'm back *po tebe i Emira* [for you and Emir].

LEJLA *Kako je nepristojan.* [Emir is being rude.]

EMIR enters.

Emire. (He glares.) Nisam znala. [I didn't know…]

SARAH *(to EMIR) Zdravo…* [Hello…]

EMIR walks quickly towards SARAH and TARIK.

LEJLA *Stani. Ne ponašaj se tako.* [Stop. You're being rude.]

He sits down at the table with his back to TARIK and SARAH.

TARIK *Lejla, pokaži sari moju sobu.* [Lejla, show Sarah my room.]

LEJLA *Da naravno izvini Zera.* [Yes, of course, I'm sorry Sarah.]

LEJLA gathers all of the luggage and heads for TARIK's old bedroom. SARAH follows, trying to help.

Dođi Zera, dođi, pokazaću ti Tarikovu sobu. Mora da si umorna, nema potrebe da sjediš i gledaš ove dvije budaletine, ja ću tebe smjestiti. [Come Sarah come, I'll show you Tarik's room. You must be tired, there's no need for you to sit there watching those two fools, I'll get you settled in.]

EMIR slams his cup down.

Poljubi brata. I ti njega. Odmah. Dođi, Zera, hajde. [Kiss your brother. Both of you. Now. Come on, Sarah, come on.]

SARAH I want subtitles.

LEJLA and SARAH exit.

TARIK *Lejla je ista mama, zar ne?* [Lejla looks just like Mama, don't you think?] How's your English, *braco* [brother]? Still good? Why did you hit me?

LEJLA lugs a couple weights out into the living room. TARIK's old bedroom has been serving as EMIR's storage/workout room. SARAH follows with a box.

SARAH Are these Emir's things?

LEJLA *Emirovo.* [Emir's things.]

SARAH starts for EMIR's room. LEJLA stops her.

Ne Zera. *(to EMIR) Emire skloni ovo.* [Emir put these away.] *(indicates for SARAH to put the box on the floor) Tu. Tu.* [Here. Here.] *Bravo Zera, Bravo. Dođi dođi.* [Come, come.]

LEJLA and SARAH exit. EMIR picks up his weights to move them.

TARIK Ah, you've been working out. I can tell. *(no response)* Why did you hit me? *(pause)* Are you gonna talk to me? Say something. *Reci nešto!* [Say something!] What's the matter? Say something. I'm not going to stand here all day. What's the matter with you? Cat got your tongue?

EMIR takes off his scarf and shows TARIK the scar on his neck.

Bože moj, Emire, šta su ti uradili? [Oh my God, Emir what did they do to you?] What did they do to you?

He reaches out to touch EMIR's throat. EMIR grabs TARIK's arm. LEJLA and SARAH enter. LEJLA is carrying EMIR's rifle.

SARAH When I left for university, my room got turned into a sewing room.

LEJLA turns, accidentally pointing the rifle at SARAH. SARAH jumps. LEJLA realizes her mistake, leans the rifle against the wall and covers it with some of the clothing SARAH has been carrying.

LEJLA *Ne brini…* [Don't worry…] *Ne. Ne. Boom Boom. Ne. Ne.*

SARAH *(to TARIK)* Oh. They have a gun.

SARAH exits back to TARIK's room. EMIR gets LEJLA's attention and reminds her to wake JASNA soon.

LEJLA *Znam.* [I know.]

EMIR asks if TARIK knows about JASNA. LEJLA shakes her head. He exits to balcony.

TARIK What happened to him? *Šta mu se dogodilo?* [What happened to him?]

LEJLA *Rat Tarik. Žao mi je… ja…* [War, Tarik. I'm sorry… I…]

TARIK *Šta?* [What?]

LEJLA *Tarik, nisam mislila, nikad nismo ni pomislili. Tako sam sretna što te vidim. Emir je bio ljut.* [Tarik. I didn't think… we never thought you'd… I'm so happy to see you. Emir has been very angry.]

TARIK Yeah I can tell he's angry.

LEJLA *Bijesan je zbog tebe. Misli da si pobjegao.* [Emir is angry at you. He thinks you ran away.]

TARIK Ran away? I didn't run away. *Nisam pobjegao, Lejla.* [I didn't run away, Lejla.]

LEJLA *Ima još nešto.* [There is something else.]

SARAH re-enters from TARIK's room carrying a bottle of Crown Royal with a bow on it.

SARAH We brought you this from home…

LEJLA *Odoh napraviti kafu.* [I'll make some coffee.]

TARIK *Ne, reci!* [No, tell me!]

LEJLA *Ne, ne razumiješ…* [No, you don't understand…]

She exits to the kitchen.

SARAH So… we probably should have called first.

TARIK Everything's fine.

SARAH I'm starting to doubt your translations. Why did your brother punch you?

TARIK Sarah, Emir got hurt in the war.

SARAH So he punched you?

TARIK No it's complicated. He can't speak.

SARAH He can't speak?

JASNA *(from EMIR's room)* Lejla!

TARIK Who is that?

TARIK and SARAH look at EMIR's door. LEJLA rushes in, trying to look casual. EMIR also enters.

LEJLA *Molim?* [Yes?]

TARIK *Ko je to?* [Who's that?]

LEJLA *Ko?* [Who?]

TARIK *U Emirovoj sobi.* [In Emir's room.]

LEJLA *Ne znam.* [I don't know.]

TARIK *Je li to neka djevojka?* [Was that a girl?] *Emire? (to SARAH)* He's hiding a girl in there.

LEJLA Tarik—

TARIK Anyone I know *braco*? Or do I have to find out for myself? *Izvini, curo. Izađi da se upoznamo.* [Sorry, girl. Come out so we can meet.] Why are you hiding her? Bring her out.

JASNA enters from EMIR's room.

JASNA Lejla—

TARIK Jasna?

EMIR closes JASNA's housecoat and kisses her. TARIK looks to LEJLA for an explanation.

LEJLA *Odoh ja po kafu.* [I'll get the coffee.]

She exits to kitchen.

SARAH *Zdravo. Ja sam Sarah Nakaš* [Hello. I'm Sarah Nakaš] from Canada.

JASNA *Jasna. Zdravo, Tarik.*

TARIK *Zdravo.*

TARIK makes a show of kissing SARAH.

LEJLA *(entering) Kafa. Hoćeš kafu?* [Coffee. Would you like coffee?]

SARAH Coffee? I'd love some, yes. *(to LEJLA)* Do you have decaf?

LEJLA hands her a cup.

Oh. Oh. Is it… espresso? Or…?

LEJLA *Turska.* [It's Turkish.]

SARAH *Turska?*

LEJLA *Da da, turska.* [Yes, yes, Turkish.]

l to r: Alena Džebo as Jasna, Dylan Trowbridge as Emir, Tanja Smoje as Lejla.
photo by Sue Balint

SARAH Oh, I thought it was—

TARIK It's Turkish!

SARAH It smells… good. Thank you.

SARAH stares at TARIK, waiting for an apology. He never notices.

JASNA *Dođi, Emire, ne smijem zakasniti.* [Come, Emir, I can't be late.]

He joins JASNA by the balcony. She applies cream to his scar.

LEJLA *Jasna radi noćnu, dobar posao.* [Jasna is working at night, a good job.]

Uncomfortable silence.

Ah, Zera? Jasna govorit engleski. [Jasna speaks English.] *Jasna… Engleski.*

SARAH Eng… English? She – you speak English…?

JASNA Yes I do.

SARAH Oh that's great.

TARIK You speak English?

JASNA A lot of things have changed since you left.

TARIK *(swearing under his breath) Pun ma ti kurac.* [My dick is tired of you.]

LEJLA *I Emir razumije engleski ali on ne može govoriti. Ne govoriti… ne može.* [Emir also understands English but he doesn't speak. He can't speak.]

SARAH Oh you speak English too… *(EMIR shows his scar.)* Oh. Right, you can't speak. I'm so sorry. I understand now about earlier. I would have anger too. *(EMIR beckons her over.)* Oh no thanks. I can see it from here. *(EMIR crosses to the table.)* I'm so sorry that happened to you. War is a terrible thing. *(EMIR lunges at SARAH, she jumps.)*

LEJLA *Emir, vazda se šali.* [He's such a joker.]

SARAH Vitamin E. That's good. I had a scar on my knee once. It's healing well, you can hardly tell…

JASNA *(to TARIK) Zašto si se vratio?* [Why did you come back?]

TARIK *Zašto ti jebeš mog brata?* [Why do you fuck my brother?]

LEJLA *Jesi li mislio ici u džamiju, Tarik?* [Tarik are you going to mosque?]

TARIK Mosque? I'm not the one who needs to go to mosque.

SARAH It is so nice to finally see Sarajevo…. We've been trying to get here for ages eh? This isn't the easiest guy to get a passport for. *(pause)* Actually, I took a course in international relations at university, that was during the war so you guys were… you know, like an entire term. I did a seminar on the truth and reconciliation hearings, the ones in South Africa… the truth and… reconciliation…. So I can just imagine what it will be like around here with yours…

JASNA *Radila je projekat o južnoj Africi.* [She did a school project about South Africa.]

LEJLA nods, confused.

How long are you staying?

SARAH Oh. Not long. It's a small house, a lovely house, very… Slavic.

LEJLA *Šta?* [What?]

JASNA *Pitam je koliko će ostati…* [I'm asking, how long are they staying…]

LEJLA *Možete ostati koliko hoćete.* [You can stay as long as you want.]

EMIR shakes his head.

TARIK She says we can stay as long as we want.

SARAH Oh thank you, that's… *(seeing EMIR's reaction)* But no. No, we shouldn't—

LEJLA *Emire, on ti je brat. (to SARAH) Da.* [Emir, he's your brother. Yes.]

SARAH Yes? Yes we can—

EMIR refuses.

No—

LEJLA *Da! Emire, on ti je brat i u ovu kuću je uvijek dobrodošao.* [Emir, he's your brother and he's always welcome in this house.]

EMIR bangs his hand down.

SARAH Okay… we don't have to stay for long.

TARIK Okay Emir, relax! *Emire* relax! I'm here, I'm here in our home, with my family – that's all that matters. When was the last time we were like this? In my mind we were always together, in here *(points to head)*, and in here *(touches heart)*, in my blood… I have a picture of us. I look at you every morning when I shave, *naša slika, ona s mamom i tatom u Neumu, mi stoji na ogledalu* [the picture of us with Mom and Dad in Neum is on my mirror], it kept me alive, it made me believe that the last five years of missing you and working my guts out hasn't been in vain. Toronto is my home now, Sarajevo is my soul, believe me – but Toronto is my home. You wouldn't believe how many Bosnians are there. *Lejla, u ulici Pejp ima cijelo naselje puno Bosanaca* [Lejla, there's an entire section on a street called Pape that's full of Bosnians] – all of Zoran Lončarević's cousins are there, Perla's entire family, *na Pejpu, ima puno trgovina u kojima možeš kupiti istu hranu kao i ovdje* [there's shops where you can buy all the food from here] …*suđuke, đezve, kafu, burek.*

When I got there I got a job as a plumber, and after three years I have my own company, two vans, seven people working for me, last year I made $110,000… *sto deset hiljada dolara* [one hundred and ten thousand dollars]. I made more money there in three years than I could have made here in fifteen – as soon as I could I applied to the government to bring you all over, it's taken years of paperwork, but the day it came through—last Friday— I bought our plane tickets over here, I've been waiting so long for it to come through, and…

I wanted to tell you all in person our great news, Sarah's pregnant, *imaćemo bebu* [we're going to have a baby]. The second I found out all I could think of was home, was here, was you all, we have to be together, I can't live like this anymore it's crazy, there's a Nakaš bank account in Toronto, every penny I've made has gone into it, it's for us, it's for when you come to Canada.

Emir, I have a job lined up for you, *Lejla, želim da budeš kraj mog djeteta. Niko mi ne bi bolje od tebe pomogao da ga odgojim* [Lejla, I can't think of any other woman I'd want around my child, raising it, than you]. And... *(turns to JASNA, then away)* Emir, your... accident... if I'd have known I would have come right here, I swear to you, but there's doctors in Canada, the best doctors. And do you know what? It's free. You want a new knee, it's free, a new hip, it's free, a new voice, a new life, it's all there...

This is our chance to start over again and I can't live without you anymore, it's been too long, *dođi sa mnom kući* [come home with me], come home with Sarah and me, let's start a new life...

JASNA I must get ready for work. *Izvinite.* [Excuse me.]

JASNA exits to bedroom.

SARAH We didn't know you had a girlfriend.

EMIR exits.

LEJLA *Emire.*

TARIK Lejla? Lejla?

LEJLA exits after EMIR. SARAH turns to TARIK, starts to gag. She runs to bathroom to throw up.

Fuck.

EMIR enters and begins throwing TARIK's clothes and suitcases out the door.

Emir, what are you doing? Come on, put those back. *Vrati to.* [Put it back.] I'm serious, Emir stop fucking around, those are Sarah's clothes.

Struggling over suitcase.

Okay, okay. Stop it. *Stani. Ovo je moja kuća.* [Stop it. This is my home.] This is my home too. Don't take your fucking problems out on me. Just because you're fucking my old girlfriend does not make you man of the house. *Ja sam ti brat* [I'm your brother] goddammit. I'm the only fucking brother you've got.

They wrestle to the ground.

Look at us. *Vidi nas.* [Look at us.] ...FUCK! Listen to me, *šta hoćeš* [what do you want]? Do you want to live like this? Are you happy? Are you happy here?

EMIR nods.

You don't look happy.

EMIR begins to leave.

Wait, wait, wait – *šta nije redu* [what's wrong]?

EMIR *(gesturing)* You abandoned me.

TARIK *Šta? Šta?* [What? What?] I don't understand what you're saying. What? What?

EMIR *(gesturing)* You sent us one letter, one letter in five years.

TARIK Yes, yes, write it down.

EMIR slams table, points to scar.

EMIR *(gesturing)* You did this to me, you. You did this.

TARIK What do you want me to do? What do you want me to do? I thought about you every night, Emir, I couldn't sleep thinking about you and Lejla – are they safe, are they all right, are they eating, are they alive, are they alive?

EMIR *(gesturing)* We needed you here. We needed you here.

TARIK I planned to come here right away, but it takes money, Emir, it's fucking expensive over there. When I was settled I sent a letter and after that it was just too difficult—

EMIR writes something on the back of the immigration papers.

I couldn't call. What was I supposed to say – I'm here in Canada cleaning sewers and shit, trying to make ends meet?

Each day that went by it got harder to come back or call you guys or send a letter, so I just kept going at it. I didn't mean to stay away for so long, it just happened that way.

EMIR *(gesturing)* Liar.

TARIK I don't understand you. Please. Why would you live like this? Not sure about water or electricity, soldiers breathing down your neck, no opportunities, no money.... The guy that did that to you? One day you'll probably end up sitting beside him on a tram and not even know it. Get out of this place, it's not the home we grew up in anymore, *nema ničeg više* [it's gone], let it go. *Sjedi, sjedi, molim te, molim te, sjedi.* [Sit, sit please, please, sit.]

EMIR sits.

Come home with me... *(TARIK hands the papers to EMIR.)* Do it for Lejla, give her a chance to be something, to be happy. Maybe you can't imagine what it's like because you've never really been anywhere else but here, *ali postoji puno više* [there is so much more].

Pause.

Emire, what's left for you here? Is it Jasna? You don't want to leave Jasna behind. Fuck. Are there no other girls in Sarajevo you can... *(EMIR starts to leave.)* Okay, okay... Emir, bring her, we'll work it out – you'll have to marry her.

Long pause. Then, an attempt at a joke...

She wouldn't be able to wear white. *(EMIR stares at TARIK.)* What? She wouldn't...

EMIR crumples up the papers, throws them at TARIK, and exits to his room. As he exits, JASNA enters.

Ahh! I worked my ass off to get these. *(to JASNA) Idi smiri ga. Dobra si u tome.* [Why don't you go and make your boyfriend happy? You're good at that.]

JASNA crosses to the door, puts on shoes.

Izvini, izvini. Izvini, Jasna. [I'm sorry, I'm sorry. I'm sorry, Jasna.]

JASNA You have no right to come here and speak our language; it is not for you anymore. You speak your English… I understand fine. I practice on foreigners and I…

JASNA is struggling with her bracelet.

TARIK *Ja ću.* [Allow me.]

TARIK takes JASNA's wrist.

JASNA I don't want your help.

He doesn't let go.

TARIK *Ja ću, ja ću.* [Allow me, allow me.] *(He closes the latch on her bracelet.)*

You look so… grown up. You look beautiful.

Sounds of SARAH vomiting off stage.

She's fine. Airplane food. You know.

JASNA No.

TARIK I wasn't ah… I didn't know you'd be—

JASNA Here? Did you think I'd just disappear? Where did you think I'd go?

TARIK Look… I…

JASNA We weren't expecting you to… drop by either.

TARIK I sent a letter. Didn't it get here?

JASNA One letter in five years. Until then we thought you were dead.

TARIK I said that I would be back – and here I am.

Sounds of SARAH vomiting.

JASNA I will bring her American food home tonight.

TARIK From your work? That'd be great. *(taking out his wallet)* How much do you—

JASNA Put your money away, please. What will she have?

TARIK Oh. Anything, a salad or something, green or—

JASNA I meant she's pregnant. *(pause)* What will she have?

TARIK It's too soon to tell…

JASNA But will it be Bosnian or Canadian? Or is it too soon to tell that too?

JASNA exits. LEJLA enters with the old UN box.

TARIK Lejla. *(pointing at the papers)* Lejla Nakaš. *Hoćeš sa mnom u Kanadu?* [Will you come to Canada?]

SARAH enters.

LEJLA *(broken English)* Zera. Thank you for bring my *braco* [brother] home.

LEJLA exits. SARAH smiles after LEJLA then sees her suitcases.

SARAH Why is my suitcase here? Did Emir do this? He's not surprised, he's angry. Actually he appears to hate us… I think there's something seriously wrong with him. And Lejla won't even stay in the same room with us. And, what's going on with you and Emir's girlfriend?

TARIK It's just the Bosnian temperament.

SARAH This is not funny. I woke up this morning in Toronto, expecting a family reunion. Baklava and family photos and stupid stories about what you did in high school, and since then I've been on a ten-hour flight with nothing that I could eat on the plane, morning sickness in a tiny bathroom in turbulence, dragging our bags uphill through the streets of a war, then we get here and your brother punches you as soon as we walk through the door, and I don't understand a goddamn word anyone's saying.

TARIK Sarah.

SARAH I'm exhausted, I'm filthy, and I'm pregnant. Say something.

TARIK C'mere. Lejla saved this for me.

SARAH What is it?

TARIK I don't know. I think it's my stuff.

TARIK opens the box and pulls out a football jersey.

Bože moj. [My God.] Sarah, this is the jersey of my favourite football club, *Žjelo. Manijaks. Jasam manijak.* I am a maniac!

(He sings.) Hajmo Bosna, Bosna, Bosna! [Let's go Bosnia, Bosnia, Bosnia!] *Hajmo Hercegovina!* [Let's go Hercegovina!]

SARAH Ssh, ssh, ssh!

TARIK pulls a Magic 8 Ball out of the UN box.

TARIK What the hell is this? This isn't mine.

SARAH Don't shake it! I had one of these once. Ask me something.

TARIK Am I a maniac?

SARAH *(reading the Magic 8 Ball)* "All signs point to yes."

TARIK Let me try. Ask me something.

SARAH pulls an engagement ring out of the box.

SARAH Is this yours?

TARIK *(reading the Magic 8 Ball)* "Definitely yes."

SARAH Really? *(putting the ring on)* It's beautiful.

TARIK Take it off. Take that off.

SARAH Okay. *(TARIK starts putting things back into the box.)* What did I do? *(no response)* This is a nightmare.

TARIK Well, fine, now you understand how I feel every time I go to your parents' house.

SARAH Don't play your immigrant card right now. That's not allowed in Sarajevo, I'm the foreigner here.

TARIK I told you I was uncomfortable every time but you could never understand why.

SARAH I never said you aren't a real trooper sitting through Christmas dinner in Milton, but my family is wonderful to you. I hate it here.

TARIK Well, I hate Milton.

SARAH You said Milton was lovely.

TARIK I was lying.

SARAH Oh, it all comes out now doesn't it?

TARIK Oh yes, I guess so.

TARIK turns to get suitcases.

SARAH We're not finished yet – don't walk away on me.

TARIK I'm just getting our goddamn suitcases.

SARAH You are. You are. You just walked away from our conversation even if you say you're just getting the suitcases. You just checked out.

TARIK Checked out? Fine, you want me to check out? Fine. I'm checking out. I'll check out of this place.

SARAH Fine. Just run away. You're a coward.

TARIK What?

SARAH You're a coward.

TARIK Don't. Don't ever say that.

SARAH I'm going to bed.

She exits.

TARIK Now who's checking out? *(to EMIR's door) Emire*, come on out. Oh fuck it. I've been waiting five years, I can wait another.... You'll have to come out eventually and I'll be waiting. Yeah, I'm a patient fucker!

TARIK sits by the balcony. Suddenly, a round of gunfire sounds and lights snap to Sniper's Alley.

ELMA Tarik!

ELMA appears and repeats the Sniper's Alley scene almost exactly as before. TARIK watches in silence.

Lejla. *Ne, Tarik... (showing him an envelope) Vidi ovo? Starci su mi nabavili lovu... deset hiljada.* [No, Tarik.... See this? My parents got the money... ten thousand.]

TARIK Elma?

Sound of gunshots and women yelling.

ELMA *Idem do cisterne, i oni će me izvući van.* [I'm getting on the water truck over there and they're taking me out.]

Ne znam. Pozdravi mi Lejlu. Reci joj da sam u redu. [I don't know. Tell Lejla goodbye. Tell her I'm safe.]

TARIK *Elma, čekaj...* [wait...]

ELMA *Poželi mi sreću.* [Wish me luck.]

ELMA runs out into the alley. Another round of shots are fired. ELMA falls, dropping the envelope beside her.

TARIK Elma!

TARIK walks up to her dead body and crouches beside her. Silence. Suddenly her arm moves.

Sranje! [Shit!]

ELMA is trying to reach the envelope, but she can't.

Elma. Elma, I... *Šta hoćeš...?* [What do you want?] This?

He picks up the envelope and hands it to her. ELMA stands, rewinds and repeats the scene again.

ELMA Tarik! Lejla. *Ne, Tarik... (showing him an envelope) Vidi ovo? Starci su mi nabavili lovu... deset hiljada.* [No, Tarik.... See this? My parents got the money... ten thousand.]

Sound of gunshots and women yelling.

Idem do cisterne, i oni će me izvući van. [I'm getting on the water truck over there and they're taking me out.]

TARIK Elma? Can you stop for a minute?

ELMA *Ne znam. Pozdravi mi Lejlu. Reci joj da sam u redu.* [I don't know. Tell Lejla goodbye. Tell her I'm safe.]

TARIK Please? Elma? Please?

ELMA *Poželi mi sreću.* [Wish me luck.]

TARIK No! Don't do it. *Čekaj.* [Wait.] Elma! *(ELMA falls again, and reaches for the envelope. He sits, far away from her.) Šta hoćeš?* [What do you want?] What do you want from me? Elma?

ELMA keeps reaching for the envelope, but can't quite get it. TARIK closes his eyes, trying to ignore her.

Blackout.

Scene Three

Lights up on JASNA at work. She is on her hands and knees scrubbing the floor.

Lights down.

Scene Four

Lights up on LEJLA.

LEJLA *Emire.*

Lights up on EMIR. They are at either end of the stage – although in reality they are right next to each other.

Ti i Tarik. [You and Tarik.]

She holds up a photo. On the other side of the stage, he receives it.

Manijaci. [Maniacs.] *(singing quietly) Hajmo Bosna, Bosna, Bosna…* [Let's go Bosnia, Bosnia, Bosnia…]

EMIR smiles and sits.

Braco te voli. [Your brother loves you.]

He looks up.

Canada… *idi Emire* [go Emir].

He shakes his head.

Doktor. [Doctor.] *(strokes her throat)*

EMIR strokes his throat.

(singing to him quietly)
Mehmeda majka budila. [Mother was waking up Mehmed.]
Ustani sine Mehmede. [Get up my son Mehmed.]

EMIR smiles and laughs. He gestures "will you go to Canada?"

LEJLA shakes her head. He asks why.

Kuća. [Home.]

Blackout.

Scene Five

The main room of the flat. Later that evening. ELMA is still reaching for the envelope. TARIK sits watching her, drinking the Crown Royal from the bottle. JASNA returns from work, carrying some boxes of food. She is unaware of ELMA.

TARIK Jasna. *Sjedi sjedi. Hajde, plavka hajde.* [Sit sit. Come here, blondie come here.] Drink with me.

She takes the bottle and drinks.

Moramo je dokrajčiti. [We've gotta finish that.] No good Bosnian goes to sleep with an open bottle.

JASNA What do you know about good Bosnians?

TARIK *(pointing to a box)* Is that for me?

JASNA *Za Saru.* [For Sarah.]

TARIK What about that one?

JASNA *Za Emira.* [For Emir.]

TARIK takes EMIR's box and eats a cookie from it.

TARIK And you, you're for Emir now too?

JASNA You told him to take care of me, so he took care of me.

JASNA turns to leave.

TARIK Wait.

He takes the boxes, she grabs for them. He puts them down, away from her. She turns to leave. He pulls her towards him, she pulls away, he pulls her back, this time spinning her into a dance.

(singing) I'm seventeen and I've never been kissed…

JASNA laughs and dances with him.

JASNA *Smanji kolače, stomak ti raste.* [Eat less sweets, your stomach's getting big.]

TARIK *Obojila si kosu, plavka.* [You coloured your hair, blondie.]

JASNA *A ti ćelaviš…* [And you're balding…]

He tries to kiss her.

Tarik, *ne.*

TARIK *Daj.* [Come on.]

JASNA *(pulling away) Ne, Tarik, stani.* [No, Tarik, stop.]

Long pause.

TARIK How's Emir?

JASNA He's very brave.

TARIK I need you to talk to him. He won't listen to me. *Pomozi mi.* [Help me.]

JASNA How can I help you?

TARIK You have to help me save him.

JASNA You're not doing this for them, you're doing this because you feel guilty. You're lucky we even talk to you.

TARIK Fuck me, all right, if none of you ever want to talk to me again, fine. *Briga me.* [I don't care.] They need this. Help me.

JASNA Help you take them from their home? To run away?

TARIK To give them a chance.

JASNA *Šansu za šta?* [A chance for what?] To start over with nothing?

TARIK I am giving them everything. A house. Money. Do you know how many people would kill for this chance? Do you know how many people they turn down every year? Jasna. Emir could get help.

JASNA So they could give him a brand new Canadian voice like yours?

TARIK If you love my brother you'll let him get help.

JASNA *Tvoj brat je sretan ovdje.* [Your brother is happy here.]

TARIK No he's not. Neither is Lejla. This isn't living. They could be more than this.

JASNA So that's what you want for them? To be ashamed of who they are?

TARIK I'm happy there. I have a better life there.

JASNA The only way to live is the North American way, every other is misery, right? Go back to your better life, with your wife who doesn't know anything about you, our life is not so bad here.

TARIK What's wrong with you? If you're jealous because I brought Sarah here, fine, I understand. This Emir thing is…

JASNA Is… is… what. It is not a thing. How dare you even think this is about us.

JASNA exits to EMIR's room.

ELMA begins reaching for the envelope again. TARIK turns back to confront her.

TARIK I get it, okay? I get the point. *(pause)* It's not my fault! You saw they were shooting and you ran out. You got shot. You died. End of story.

ELMA reaches for the envelope again.

Oh for chrissakes it's right in front of you.

He kicks the envelope to her. She stands up, rewinds and repeats the scene again.

Šta hoćeš od mene? [What do you want from me?]

ELMA Tarik! Lejla. *Ne, Tarik… (showing him an envelope) Vidi ovo? Starci su mi nabavili lovu… deset hiljada.* [No, Tarik…. See this? My parents got the money… ten thousand.]

Sounds of gunfire and women shouting.

Idem do cisterne, i oni će me izvući van. [I'm getting on the water truck over there and they're taking me out.]

TARIK *(while she continues)* Elma. Elma! You're really pissing me off. *Stani stani.* Stop stop. Don't Elma. Don't do it!

ELMA *Ne znam. Pozdravi mi Lejlu. Reci joj da sam u redu.* [I don't know. Tell Lejla goodbye. Tell her I'm safe.]

Poželi mi sreću. [Wish me luck.]

ELMA runs out into the alley. TARIK grabs her.

TARIK Stop it!

She tries to push past him. The struggle escalates into a full-out brawl. Eventually TARIK is on top of her, beating her. He is screaming "Leave! Me! Alone!" Eventually ELMA stops moving. A long pause.

Okay. Okay.

He starts to walk away. ELMA reaches for the envelope. TARIK runs from the house.

Lights down.

Scene Six

Lights up on EMIR. He sits by the balcony, wrapped in a blanket.

EMIR *(voiceover)* I can't sleep.
I can't sleep
I can't speak.
I wake up screaming
But nobody hears me.

JASNA enters. She starts changing for bed. She doesn't see EMIR watching her.

Nobody hears.

Over there I am nothing I have no story. Here I have survived. Here I am yours. Jasna, my Jasna, who will you be in that strange country? What will you become? You with your beauty and your English. Will I disappear? Yes, I will be nothing to you. A man from nowhere with no words to caress you.

l to r: Alena Džebo as Jasna, Dylan Trowbridge as Emir.
photo by Chris Gallow

JASNA notices EMIR.

Do you still love him, Jasna? Do you still love him?

When he was dead, it was okay. You found me. We both loved him dead. But alive… alive. Do you love him Jasna? Did you ever stop?

JASNA and EMIR move to each other. They perform a brief movement piece and return to the balcony together.

Do you hate me Jasna? Do you hate me for not being him?

Oh Jasna if I could speak, all the things I would say. With one word I'd become a river and reflect the lovely secrets buried deep within your soul. Say something. Say something. Say something. Say something. Say something. Say something…

Blackout.

Scene Seven

Lights up on SARAH in bed.

SARAH Move…
Move…
Not yet? Don't worry.

This is the room your daddy grew up in. Your papa? Your daddy. This was his room. His home. *Kućo. Kuća, Kući? Kući. Kuća.* Where is he?

Sometimes you have to stand by someone you love even though they're being a royal pain in the you-know-where.

Tomorrow we will go down to Bahshartchia where the old women sell birdseed. I'll buy a cupful and put it on my belly. And you can meet the birds. Daddy says there are so many birds that when they fly it looks like a snowstorm. Where did he go? There's a fountain here where the water is always flowing and, if you drink from it, you are forever bound to Sarajevo. No matter where you go you will always have to return.

I'm not going to drink from it, don't worry.

This is your family. This is your family too.

She begins to sing "Blue Eyes" by Fats Waller.

TARIK begins to walk around the perimeter of the stage. He is climbing to the top of a hill overlooking Sarajevo. He sings with SARAH though they are unaware of each other.

Near the end of the song SARAH disappears. TARIK sings the final line alone.

TARIK arrives at the top of the hill, out of breath. It is very late at night. He attempts to catch his breath. Suddenly, out of nowhere, a UN Soldier appears.

SOLDIER That's quite the hill.

TARIK *Jebote.* [Fuck.]

SOLDIER *Ja sam Bill.* [I am Bill.]

TARIK Where did you come from?

SOLDIER Canada.

TARIK Really? I'm from Toronto.

SOLDIER Fuckin' eh! St. John. My little brother's in Toronto.

TARIK What are you doing here?

SOLDIER Babysitting with a gun. Fucking waste of time. If I have to be away from home it should be somewhere I can at least make a difference. Africa, wherever. You a tourist or something?

TARIK Or something.

SOLDIER Right on. Fuckin' eh.

TARIK It's a beautiful view, eh? The city down below all lit up. From here you could almost believe there was never a war.

SOLDIER Not me. Hey, you want the tour? *(pointing)* Bridge, river, bridge, bridge, Turks, Serbs… mosque. Potholes, bullet holes landmines. And that's everything. Now you can go back home.

TARIK When are you finished here?

SOLDIER We'll never be finished here. The minute you turn your back, they're trying to kill each other. You're a good guy, let me ask you something.

TARIK Shoot.

SOLDIER Sit down. When I walk through the streets of the old city on my day off, they look at me like I'm the enemy. Beautiful girls, kids, old men in shops. When we first got here, we were heroes, you know? We stopped a war, we saved innocent people. This place looked like hell. Not like Europe, like hell. So, are they mad because we came too late? Or are they mad because they want to finish it off and we won't let them?

TARIK Maybe they just want to forget.

SOLDIER It'll never happen. This place is scarred, bullet holes in buildings, whole soccer fields are graveyards. These people will never forget.

TARIK It's hard for them.

SOLDIER That's right. The ones that got out – they're the lucky ones. If I had my way, I'd get them all out of here, give 'em a fresh start. They need our help.

TARIK They may not want it but they need it.

SOLDIER It's our responsibility to do what's best for them.

TARIK It's our responsibility to do what's best for them.

SOLDIER That's right. That old woman over there? Every day she lays a flower on the road down in the city… our translator told us her daughter was found dead there. Now she's has nothing. She's a beggar.

TARIK What woman?

SOLDIER Over there, begging for change.

TARIK I can't see her.

SOLDIER She's just over there.

TARIK *(walking to where SOLDIER pointed)* Where? *(turns to SOLDIER who has disappeared)* Buddy? Where…? *(turns back and the old WOMAN has appeared, motioning to him)* *Šta hoćeš? Hoćeš pare? Ovo?* [What do you want? Want money? This?]

The old WOMAN refuses his money. A water canister appears in her hands. She hands it to TARIK.

No. no. no.

Light snaps to Sniper's Alley. Gunshots as before. ELMA re-appears. The old woman disappears.

ELMA Tarik!

TARIK Elma. Lejla's waiting for you.

ELMA Lejla.

TARIK Back at our place. You need water? Where's your canister, I'll—

ELMA No, Tarik… *(showing him an envelope)* See this? My parents got the money… ten thousand.

TARIK What?

Two women enter with their canisters and begin crossing. Another round of gunfire. One woman freezes in fear. Everyone yells at her to keep going. The first woman doubles back, grabs the frozen woman, they complete their crossing and exit.

ELMA I'm getting on the truck over there and they're taking me out.

TARIK Where are they taking you?

ELMA I don't know. *(pause)* Tell Lejla goodbye. Tell her I'm safe.

TARIK I will, of course. Elma, be careful.

ELMA Wish me luck.

TARIK Good luck.

ELMA runs out into the alley. Another round of shots are fired. ELMA falls, dropping the envelope beside her.

Elma!

TARIK starts after her. Gunshots force him back. He runs to her again and kneels to help her. She reaches for the envelope. He sees it, picks it up and looks back at ELMA. He looks at the envelope and decides to take it. He runs.

Light returns to hilltop.

(out of breath from running) I took her money.
I took her money.
I took her money.
I took her money.
I took her money.

The SOLDIER re-appears.

SOLDIER You took her money?

TARIK I took her money.

SOLDIER You took her money.

The old WOMAN re-appears.

WOMAN *Uzeo si joj pare?* [You took her money?]

TARIK *(to WOMAN) Trebaju moju pomoć.* [They need my help.]

WOMAN *Trebaju tvoju pomoć?* [They need your help?]

TARIK *(to WOMAN)* They need my help.

SOLDIER They need your help.

WOMAN *Uzeo si joj pare?* [You took her money?]

TARIK *(to SOLDIER)* They need my help.

SOLDIER They need your help.

TARIK *(to SOLDIER)* I took her money.

SOLDIER You took her money.

TARIK *(to SOLDIER)* They need my help.

SOLDIER They need your help.

WOMAN *Trebaju tvoju pomoč?* [They need your help?]

TARIK *(to WOMAN) Trebaju moju pomoć.* [They need my help.]

WOMAN *Uzeo si joj pare.* [You took her money.]

TARIK *(to WOMAN) Uzeo sam joj pare.* [I took her money.]

WOMAN *Uzeo si joj pare.* [You took her money.]

TARIK *(to WOMAN) Uzeo sam joj pare.* [I took her money.]

WOMAN Uzeo si joj pare. [You took her money.]

TARIK *(to WOMAN)* I did the right thing.

SOLDIER You did the right thing.

TARIK *(to SOLDIER)* I did the right thing.

SOLDIER You did the right thing.

WOMAN *Dobro si uradio?* [You did the right thing?]

TARIK *(to WOMAN) Dobro sam uradio.* [I did the right thing.]

SOLDIER You took her money?

WOMAN *Trebaju tvoju pomoć.* [They need your help.]

SOLDIER *Trebaju tvoju pomoć.* [They need your help.]

WOMAN You took her money?

TARIK *(to WOMAN)* I did the right thing.

SOLDIER You did the right thing.

WOMAN *Useo si joj pare.* [You took her money.]

TARIK *(to SOLDIER)* I did the right thing.

SOLDIER You did the right thing.

WOMAN *Useo si joj pare.* [You took her money.]

TARIK *(to SOLDIER)* I did the right thing.

SOLDIER You did the right thing.

WOMAN *Useo si joj pare.* [You took her money.]

TARIK I did the right thing.
I did the right thing.

The SOLDIER and old WOMAN fall.

I did the right thing!

Blackout.

Scene Eight

The main room of the flat. Early the next morning. LEJLA is making burek at the table. As she works she starts to sing.

LEJLA (*singing*) *Tekla voda,* [Water's flowing,]
Tekla voda što nas dijeli, [The water that separates us,]
Odnijela je [It took away]
Odnijela je život cijeli, [It took away our whole lives,]
Tekla voda… [Water's flowing…]

EMIR (*singing offstage*) *Sada mi se javljaš mila…* [Now you're here my dear…]

LEJLA stops and listens. Silence. She continues working.

TARIK (*singing offstage*) *Sada kad sam zadnja žed…* [Now when I'm your last resort…]

She stops again. EMIR and TARIK enter as she resumes singing.

LEJLA (*singing*) *Da ja pređem preko svega…* [You want me to forget about everything…]
Preko čega nećo preć. [But I cannot forget.]

Smiling, she touches EMIR's throat. He sings.

EMIR (*singing*) *Sada mi se javljaš mila…* [Now you're here my dear…]

LEJLA embraces EMIR. They all sing and dance together.

ALL (*singing*) *Kad ti je u duši lom,* [When your heart is breaking,]
Postao sam zadnji čovjek, [I've become the last man,]
Za tebe na svijetu tom. [For you in this world.]

TARIK spins LEJLA. As she spins, the brothers disappear. LEJLA is left alone. She returns to her burek. SARAH enters from bedroom. A nervous pause.

LEJLA	*Dobro jutro…* *Zera…*	**SARAH**	Good morning… Lejla.

Žao mi je za sinoć… [I'm sorry for last night…]

SARAH I'm so sorry? I don't—

LEJLA *Gdje je Tarik?* [Where is Tarik?]

SARAH Oh, Tarik? Tarik must have gone out. He was gone, when I woke up so… he must be the early bird…. Early. Bird.

SARAH taps her wrist and flaps her arms. LEJLA imitates her.

LEJLA *Sjedi… sjedi…* [Sit… sit…]

SARAH sits at the table.

Jesi li spavala…? [Did you sleep…?]

SARAH Did I… did I sleep well? Yes, thank you. Did you… sleep… well?

LEJLA *Da, spavala sam dobro. Hoćeš kafu?* [Yes I slept well. Would you like some coffee?]

SARAH Uh… no. No thanks, I'm good. *(pause)* You don't know where he went do you?

LEJLA nods, smiles. SARAH moves towards the balcony to look out the window.

There's no reason to worry, right? It's just…. It's just… I don't know. It's weird for him to be back here, right? It's weird. It's just… it's very intense and we didn't… I didn't expect to be… I'm just, I'm freaking out because I'm pregnant. And I haven't slept properly in 48 hours. And I'm worried. I'm just… I'm worried about him. And I'm worried about my baby and I don't know if what I'm… I'm just… I'm sorry, I'm sorry, I just, I'm sorry…

SARAH bursts into tears. Confused, LEJLA moves to comfort her.

LEJLA Oh, sshh… *(She tries to calm SARAH down by having her roll the pastry.) Zera vidi… možeš mi pomoći… možeš mi pomoći… valjaš… valjaš… valjaš…* [Sarah look… you can help me… you can help me… roll… roll… roll…]

Uzmi malo bureka… (offering her some burek) osjećat ćeš se bolje. [Try a little burek… it makes you feel better.]

SARAH Is this meat? I don't eat meat.

LEJLA Jasna. Jasna. Jasna!

JASNA enters.

Jasna molim te, ne razumijem je, dođe žena, plače k'o godina… [Jasna please, I don't understand her, she just came in and burst into tears…]

JASNA What's wrong?

LEJLA *(urgently offering more burek) Dobar burek. Dobar. Njam njam!* [Good burek. Good. Yum yum!]

JASNA Lejla's burek is best in Sarajevo.

LEJLA *Šta?* [What?]

JASNA *Kažem joj da praviš najbolji burek u Sarajevu.* [I said your burek is the best in Sarajevo.]

LEJLA *Mamin burek je bio najbolji na svijetu.* [My mother's burek was the best in the whole world.]

SARAH *Ne jebem meso. (Shocked, JASNA and LEJLA stop.) Ne jebem meso. (JASNA and LEJLA laugh.)*

JASNA You don't fuck meat?

SARAH No. No. Eat. Eat. *Ne jebem meso.*

LEJLA *Jedem. (She mimes eating.) Jebem. (She mimes sex.)*

They all laugh.

SARAH No, no, I don't fuck meat. I don't eat meat either. Vegetarian.

LEJLA *A beba je li ona vegetarijanac?* [Is the baby vegetarian?]

LEJLA exits laughing.

SARAH When he's older he can make a decision himself.

JASNA He?

SARAH …herself.

JASNA She?

SARAH I don't know.

JASNA But for now, you must keep healthy yourself.

SARAH I am healthy. I'm very healthy.

JASNA But you look pale.

SARAH My mom is German.

LEJLA enters with a child's T-shirt.

LEJLA *Tarikovo. Za bebu.* [Tarik's. For the baby.]

SARAH Oh this was Tarik's?

LEJLA *(referring to TARIK's height as a child) Ovoliki je bio.* [He was this big.]

JASNA *(referring to TARIK's penis size) Bogami je bio manji.* [It was smaller.]

LEJLA *Nemoj, bona.* [Don't, girl.]

SARAH What?

JASNA Okay, sorry. Here's the story. His father took him to see his first game. Tarik wore this shirt. He was so small and skinny as a boy, it looked like he was wearing a dress. He was running around yelling "*Ja sam Manijak!*"

LEJLA *Pitaj je kako je upoznala Tarika.* [Ask her how she met Tarik.]

JASNA *Ne želim to da je pitam.* [I don't want to ask her that.]

LEJLA *Ne budi smiješna, ona je naša sad.* [Don't be silly. She's family now.]

JASNA She wants to know… how you and Tarik met.

SARAH Well, I ducked into a bar to get out of the snow. And I stayed for a drink. And he offered to buy me the next one.

JASNA *(to LEJLA) Upoznali su se u kafiću.* [They met in a bar.]

LEJLA laughs.

SARAH He is very smooth.

JASNA You didn't tell him to go away?

SARAH No, it was… I thought it was romantic.

LEJLA Oh, *romantično.* [Oh, romantic.]

SARAH He proposed to me that night. And every night after that for two months. Until I said yes.

LEJLA *Šta, pričaj!* [What, tell me!]

JASNA *Prosio ju je svake noći dok nije pristala.* [He proposed to her every night until she accepted.]

LEJLA *Bože!* [Goodness!]

JASNA *Uvijek je bio uporan gad.* [He always was a stubborn ass.] I'm going to eat this. *(She takes SARAH's burek.)*

SARAH How did you and Emir meet?

JASNA I was a friend of the family.

LEJLA *Šta*? [What?]

JASNA *Pita kako znam Emira.* [She asked how I met Emir.]

LEJLA smiles uncomfortably.

SARAH You were Tarik's girlfriend weren't you?

LEJLA *Šta*? [What?]

Silence. LEJLA smiles at SARAH, gathers the burek supplies and exits.

SARAH I'm sorry.

JASNA It's okay.

SARAH Emir seems like a great guy…

JASNA He is.

SARAH Sometimes things work out for the best. I'd really love for all of you to come home with us.

JASNA You want more Maniacs running around your house?

SARAH I am an only child. I always wanted a big family. Can I ask you something? Why is Emir so mad? Why does nobody want to come home with us? Tarik loves you all so much, he worked so hard to keep his promise to bring you all to Canada.

JASNA That's not what he promised.

SARAH What?

JASNA How much do you really know?

SARAH About what?

JASNA About them, and me?

SARAH He's my husband.

JASNA Then you know how he got to Canada.

SARAH Yes. He escaped.

JASNA From what?

SARAH From the war.

JASNA From us.

A change in the lighting. Suddenly it is spring, 1993. EMIR enters from his bedroom.

Because JASNA is telling the following story to SARAH, everyone speaks in English (though in reality they would all be speaking Bosnian). SARAH remains on stage and watches the scene play out.

EMIR Jasna, is Tarik back yet?

JASNA Not yet.

EMIR I'll go find him.

JASNA Okay.

EMIR *(exiting)* Bye.

JASNA *(to SARAH)* Tarik had been gone for more than two hours. We were starting to worry.

LEJLA enters singing "Seventeen and Never Been Kissed." JASNA starts putting on her make-up.

LEJLA *(showing candy)* Look what Elma gave me.

JASNA Oh, nice.

LEJLA You're pretty. *(She starts putting on some of JASNA's lipstick.)*

JASNA That's your colour! Let me help you with this. *(takes lipstick)* Go like this. *(puts lipstick on her and holds up mirror)* Have you ever French kissed?

LEJLA Yeah.

JASNA Then I don't have to show you.

LEJLA Maybe your way is different than mine. Go ahead.

JASNA Oh no, you're an expert.

LEJLA No. Yeah, I mean. Come on, show me.

JASNA *(taking a cup)* Pretend this is him. And... then...

JASNA puts a candy in the cup and demonstrates a French kiss. She hands the cup to LEJLA to try.

LEJLA Will you still be here when Elma gets here?

JASNA When is she getting here?

LEJLA Soon. You have to teach her too. Your way is not that bad.

JASNA That's it... roll, roll... change, change... perfect.

LEJLA continues. TARIK and EMIR enter with the box from the UN, catching her in the act. They laugh and make kissing noises.

LEJLA Leave me alone!

TARIK runs over to tease her.

TARIK Oh, I'm sorry. I thought you were my little sister. Jasna, who's your friend? *(tickling her)* She's just a kid!

LEJLA I'm seventeen.

TARIK *(singing)* ...and never been kissed.

JASNA I was worried about you.

TARIK Emir's so ugly he scares all the snipers away.

JASNA No he's not!

TARIK But I got it…

They gather around the box. TARIK pulls a flower from behind the box and gives it to JASNA.

JASNA From the UN?

TARIK Yep. They told me to give it to the prettiest girl in Sarajevo.

TARIK opens the box and starts distributing the items.

Another grey blanket. Gloves. Bandages? Powdered milk… no one here drinks powdered milk…

Reaching back in, TARIK takes out the Magic 8 Ball.

What the hell.

JASNA What's that?

TARIK It's a toy.

JASNA It says… "Outlook not so good."

LEJLA What does that mean?

EMIR Like… your future doesn't look so good.

TARIK Why don't they send us something we can use? I hate having to smile and say thank you for this crap.

JASNA Okay, I know…

TARIK We need money. If I'm going to be a beggar, send us some money, goddamn it.

EMIR Yeah and a big plane to fly us all out of here.

Suddenly, a power surge. The lights snap on, as does the radio – Whitney Houston's superhit "How Will I Know?" plays. All three stop. The power snaps back off. They groan and sink back into their chairs.

Another power surge. They freeze and wait as before. The light stays on. EMIR and LEJLA jump into action, exiting for the kitchen.

Get to work! **LEJLA** Let's go!

JASNA starts to jump into action.

TARIK Jasna wait. I got this today. Do you know what it is?

TARIK holds out a small box with an engagement ring in it.

JASNA It's your momma's ring.

TARIK Jasna, I promise, when all this is over and I can provide for you like a good husband should, when it's safe for us to raise a family in this home. Then. Then, I'm going to ask you to marry me. But I want you to keep this until then.

LEJLA returns with the vacuum and starts vacuuming everything in sight. EMIR enters with the water canister.

EMIR We have no water.

TARIK Didn't you get water last night?

EMIR I forgot.

TARIK It was your turn.

EMIR I know. I'll go now.

TARIK No, no, no. It's bad out there today. I'll go.

EMIR tosses TARIK the canister.

LEJLA Tarik, go get the water. Elma and I want to make burek.

TARIK Okay, fine. *(He kisses JASNA.)* I'll be right back. *(to EMIR)* Take care of my girls.

He exits. LEJLA vacuums her way offstage. EMIR heads to the kitchen. JASNA and SARAH remain on stage. Lighting shifts. We return to 1998.

JASNA That was the last time we saw him.

SARAH I thought you all knew he was leaving. I thought it was planned. So he just ran away? Why didn't he—

TARIK enters from outside. He has a flower for SARAH.

JASNA Ask your husband.

SARAH Tarik.

TARIK Sarah.

SARAH We have to talk.

TARIK I know. Sarah, I know… I know… yesterday didn't go like we hoped it would. But I straightened things out – everything will be okay now. Sarah, I'm sorry about yesterday okay? *(He gives SARAH the flower. To JASNA:)* Jasna, we got off to a rough start yesterday and I apologize. I know that you and Emir really love each other – that's all that matters – I want you to come to Canada with us. I'm okay with it. It's all okay. The past is the past. (*takes out papers)* Jasna I got you these. Papers for you to come to Canada. Just fill it all out. It will be fine.

JASNA You really don't understand, Tarik. I'm not coming. Nobody wants to come.

TARIK Listen—

JASNA You listen. We don't care about Canada. We don't care about how much money you made or how hard it was. All we wanted was for you to come home. We wasted five years waiting for you. We've moved on. We don't need you anymore. You aren't part of the family.

TARIK It's my family not your family. You're just the girlfriend here.

JASNA I belong here. This is my home.

TARIK No, it's my home. I'm the oldest son, so when Papa died the deed passed on to me. I own this house.

JASNA So what?

TARIK So what? I'm selling it.

JASNA No you're not.

TARIK This morning I went to the agency. I put it up for sale.

SARAH You did what?

JASNA *Emire!*

LEJLA and EMIR enter.

TARIK *(to SARAH)* They need my help. If this is the only way to get them a better life, then so be it.

SARAH You can't force them.

JASNA *(to EMIR) Prodaće kuću.* [He's selling the house.]

LEJLA *Šta se dešava?* [What is going on?]

JASNA *(to LEJLA) Prodaće kuću.* [He's selling the house.]

LEJLA *Šta će uraditi?* [What is he going to do?]

JASNA *(to LEJLA) Prodaće kuću.* [He's selling the house.]

TARIK *Odlučio sam.* [I've made a decision.] I'm the head of this family. It's my responsibility to do what's best for you. *Prodaću kuću.* [I'm selling this house.] You will come to Canada. All of you. Whether you like it or not.

SARAH	I don't agree with this. I don't agree. Go back and stop this. Tarik, you can stop this right?	**JASNA**	*Ne daj mu Emire. Zaustavi ga.* [Don't allow this Emir. Stop him.] *(to TARIK) Samo preko mene mrtve.* [Over my dead body.]	**LEJLA**	*Šta će uraditi?* [What is he going to do?] *Šta će uraditi?* [What is he going to do?]

TARIK *Kraj priče.* [End of discussion.] It's done. I'm selling the house. There's nothing you can do about it. So you better start packing.

SARAH	You can't do this.	**LEJLA**	*Šta ćeš uraditi?* [What are you going to do?]
TARIK	Yes I can.	**JASNA**	*(to EMIR) Idi u agenciju i prekini ovo.* [Go to the agency and stop this.]

SARAH	This isn't for them. This is for you. Lejla, I'm sorry. I didn't know. We'll get your house back.	**TARIK**	You can't stop it. It's my house. Emir, if you want somewhere to live, you can come to Canada.
		JASNA	Sarah, there's your hero. I'm sorry I had to tell you, but it's important you know the truth.
SARAH	Emir, will you tell her we'll get your house back?	**TARIK**	What did you tell her?
		JASNA	I told her you ran away. I told her you're a coward.
		TARIK	No I'm not. Sarah I'm not. Jasna, what did you tell her? What did she tell you?
		SARAH	You abandoned them.
		TARIK	*(to JASNA)* Are you happy now? Are you fucking happy?
JASNA	*(to EMIR) Hoćeš li išta uraditi?* [Are you going to do anything at all?]	**SARAH**	Give them their house back.

LEJLA *Da se bogdo nisi vratio.* [I wish you had never come back.]

LEJLA runs at TARIK and starts hitting him.

TARIK *Stani, stani, stani!* [Stop, stop, stop!]

TARIK pushes LEJLA to the floor. Silence. EMIR exits.

JASNA *Vidi šta radiš!* [See what you're doing!]

SARAH I don't know who you are.

TARIK Lejla.

EMIR returns carrying his gun.

What are you going to do with that? Are you going to shoot me? Shoot me then.

EMIR motions for TARIK to go.

I'm not leaving.

EMIR points the rifle at TARIK.

Go on, do it. Shoot me *braco*. Shoot me. If that's going to make you feel—

He shoots him. TARIK falls to the ground, clutching his arm and dropping the immigration papers.

Lights snap to "Sniper's Alley."

I've been shot. I've been shot.

ELMA appears and runs to TARIK.

ELMA Tarik! Stay down! Are you okay? Hold on to me. Keep moving. Come on. Come on. Are you okay?

ELMA picks up the immigration papers.

TARIK I've been shot. I've been shot.

ELMA *(dragging TARIK to the balcony)* You're going to be okay, you're going to be okay. *(tying a rag around his arm)* Put this on. It'll be okay.

TARIK Okay.

ELMA *(handing him the papers)* These are yours.

TARIK Yeah.

ELMA What are they?

TARIK They're immigration papers for my family.

ELMA Are you getting out?

TARIK Yeah, I'm taking my family to Canada.

ELMA That's great! They must have been expensive.

Pause.

TARIK Elma, I'm sorry I took the money.

ELMA What?

TARIK Your money. Elma, I'm sorry I took your money.

ELMA I don't have any money. I have to go.

ELMA prepares to cross the alley as before.

TARIK No...

ELMA Wish me luck.

TARIK No, no, no, no, no...

She runs into the alley and is shot.

ELMA! I didn't mean to take your money. I thought you were dead. Elma, I thought you were dead.

(ELMA stands, rewinds and repeats.) No, no, no, no, don't.

(to LEJLA) I didn't mean it, Lejla. I didn't know she was alive.

(to ELMA) I didn't know you were alive.

(ELMA is shot.) Elma! Okay, okay, okay, I knew you were alive and I took your money anyway... Elma, please. I knew you were alive.

(ELMA stands, rewinds and repeats. TARIK goes to EMIR.) I knew she was alive but I took her money anyway. Make her stop. Stop. Stop her. Make her stop! Emir stop her!

(ELMA is shot.) Elma! If I could do it again I wouldn't leave you there. Elma, if I could do it again. If I could do it again.

(ELMA stands and rewinds. TARIK speaks to LEJLA.) I shouldn't have left you.

(to EMIR) I was scared.

(crumpling to the ground) I made a mistake. I made a mistake. I made a mistake.

Lighting returns to that of the Nakaš flat. TARIK is now lying on the ground, holding his arm again. His family watches him. ELMA has disappeared.

Water... going for water... I was getting water. Elma. She was getting out. I watched her get shot. She was still alive.

I went to help her but I took her money and I ran away. I thought if I tried to bring you to Canada she would go away. But she won't go away. She won't go away. She won't go away.

Blackout.

Scene Nine

Lights up on EMIR as he finishes praying. He rolls up his prayer rug and sits on the balcony watching the city. SARAH and JASNA enter – during the scene they are re-setting the kitchen table and chairs.

SARAH This is my first real trip anywhere. I mean I've been to Ottawa to visit my grandmother but.... The only other place I've been is Iowa. I went in grade 8 on a school trip

l to r: Christopher Morris as Tarik, Holly Lewis as Sarah, Dylan Trowbridge as Emir, Tanja Smoje as Lejla, Alena Džebo as Jasna.
photo by Sue Balint

with the band. I played clarinet. We were invited to play in a youth concert with student bands from all over the world. It was like youth Olympics for woodwinds. They have a Fair there, in Iowa, where you can go see a cow carved out of butter. The butter cow. It's the best thing about the fair. That was years ago but apparently now they have a whole family. Carved out of butter. Seriously. Just butter.

(pause) I'm leaving him. *(pause)* I'm leaving him.

Pause.

JASNA There is a story in Bosnia about a great theft that happened a long time ago. Someone stole State money, so Paša needed to lay blame. He wouldn't be happy until the guilty ones were found and executed. He sent out his men who found some strangers, seven brothers, moving through the mountains near Sarajevo, and they were brought back to Paša for judgment.

Paša called the first brother before him and said to him, "Confess to your crime and I will spare your life." "I have committed no crime," the brother answered, and Paša ordered his throat slit. One after another, Paša called all the brothers before him. Each was made the same offer: "Confess to your crime and I will spare your life," until he called the last brother. "Confess to your crime and I will spare your life." The last brother answered, "All my brothers died before me for nothing. I go to my death as innocent as they. Send out your men. They will find the guilty one crossing the river with the money hidden in a bag of oats."

Paša killed the seventh brother.

Soon after, the guards arrived with a prisoner and a bag of oats. The bag was set before Paša, who found at the bottom, the stolen money.

Paša built a grave—

SARAH The Grave of the Seven Brothers.

JASNA As a reminder of his own crime against them. To remember his quick judgment. To remember to listen.

l to r: Christopher Morris as Tarik, Holly Lewis as Sarah.
photo by Chris Gallow

SARAH Am I one of the brothers or the Paša? Or am I the guy with the bag of oats escaping over the river?

LEJLA enters. She takes off her shoes then crosses to SARAH and JASNA.

JASNA *(to LEJLA) Kako je on?* [How is he?]

TARIK enters. His arm is in a sling.

TARIK *(to JASNA)* I didn't… Emire look… *(takes immigration papers out of his coat)* Lejla… *(Pause. He looks at each of them and rips up the papers.)* I understand.

TARIK attempts to put the papers on the table but drops them. Pause. He kneels to pick them up. EMIR crosses to TARIK, picks up the papers for him, helps his brother up, then sits down at the table with JASNA and LEJLA. TARIK steps back and watches his family. Eventually he begins to sing.

Kad procvatu behari [When the blossoms bloom]
Kad dunjaluk zamiri [When the world becomes fragile]
Duša čeženjom procvili [The soul cries with longing]
Davno smo se rastali [We have parted a long time ago]
Allah Allah-hak Allah [In the name of God…]
Allah Allah đel-Allah
Allah—

SARAH appears wearing her coat. She carries the suitcases and TARIK's coat over to him. She stands beside TARIK and holds his hand. TARIK stops singing. Pause.

SARAH Tarik, it's snowing.

TARIK It is.

SARAH helps TARIK put on his coat.

SARAH Come home.

SARAH takes a few steps and turns to look back at TARIK. She nods for him to follow. He takes a last look at his family, picks up his suitcase and follows her. The sound of coins falling.

Lights fade.

About Theatrefront

Theatrefront is dedicated to stretching the boundaries of the human experience through theatre. Founded by Artistic Director Daryl Cloran, Theatrefront's ensemble of artists crosses borders to create unique dramatic work. We cross geographic borders to develop new work in collaboration with artists from other countries. We cross borders between artistic mediums to create theatre infused with music and movement. Theatrefront's work is self-devised and created collaboratively by the ensemble – a core group of theatre professionals who risk, innovate and experiment together.

From our first collective creation, the Dora-nominated *fforward*, Theatrefront has become synonymous with theatre that challenges and inspires audiences with a uniquely Canadian perspective. *RETURN (The Sarajevo Project)* is the first of many international co-creations for Theatrefront. The company has already begun work on collaborations in South Africa and Iceland.

www.theatrefront.com